ACTIVE
CITIZENSHIP
TODAY

Building Bridges to People Different from You

Jackie F. Stanmyre

Cavendish
Square

New York

Published in 2018 by Cavendish Square Publishing, LLC
243 5th Avenue, Suite 136, New York, NY 10016

Copyright © 2018 by Cavendish Square Publishing, LLC

First Edition

Library of Congress Cataloging-in-Publication Data

Names: Stanmyre, Jackie F.
Title: Building bridges to people different from you / Jackie F. Stanmyre.
Description: New York : Cavendish Square Publishing, 2018. | Series: Active citizenship today | Includes bibliographical references and index.
Identifiers: ISBN 9781502629128 (pbk.) | ISBN 9781502629142 (library bound) | ISBN 9781502629135 (6 pack) | ISBN 9781502629159 (ebook)
Subjects: LCSH: Individual differences--Juvenile literature. | Ethnicity--Juvenile literature. | Interpersonal relations--Juvenile literature. | Respect for persons--Juvenile literature. | Conduct of life--Juvenile literature. | Similarity (Psychology)--Juvenile literature. | Individuality--Juvenile literature. | Toleration--Juvenile literature. | Multiculturalism--Juvenile literature.
Classification: LCC BF723.I56 S737 2018 | DDC 158.2--dc23

Editorial Director: David McNamara
Editor: Fletcher Doyle
Copy Editor: Nathan Heidelberger
Associate Art Director: Amy Greenan
Designer: Joe Parenteau
Production Coordinator: Karol Szymczuk
Photo Research: J8 Media

The photographs in this book are used by permission and through the courtesy of: Cover FatCamera/E+/Getty Images; p. 4 Win McNamee/Getty Images; p. 6 Jonathan Kim/The Image Bank/Getty Images; p. 7 nano/iStock; p. 8 Richard Lewisohn/DigitalVision/Getty Images; p. 9 asiseeit/iStock; p. 10, 11, 15, 26 bottom FatCamera/iStock; p. 12 Don Mason/Blend Images/Getty Images; p. 14 Corbis/Getty Images; p. 16 Anthony Asael/Art in All of Us/Corbis News/Getty Images; p. 18 EikoTsuttiy/iStock; p. 19 Juanmonino/Vetta/Getty Images; p. 20 PeopleImages/iStock; p. 23 estivillml/iStock; p. 24 top David I. Andersen/The Plain Dealer/AP Photo; p. 24 bottom Jim West/Alamy Stock Photo; p. 25 Ron Bailey/E+/Getty Images; p. 26 top Dmytro Zinkevych/Shutterstock.com.

Printed in the United States of America

CONTENTS

Differences Are Special

All children are special. Some children look or behave differently than others. Some children who are different feel separate from other kids.

All children need to know they are special. This includes children who look and speak differently than you. This includes children who wear different clothing.

Opposite: All children should be made to feel special.

Children with different ethnicities can be friends.

Race

Some children in your neighborhood come from different backgrounds. Their families came from different places. These children may look different from you. They have a different **ethnicity**.

Here is an example. A child who is African American may have darker skin. A child whose family is originally from Ireland may have lighter skin. These children have different ethnicities. They are both special.

It can be fun to have friends of different ethnicities. You can learn about other **cultures**.

Sometimes it is hard for children who look different from others. If most of the children in a classroom have lighter skin, a child with darker skin may feel left out. It is important to let all children know they are beautiful. Everyone should be included.

Religious Dress

Another way children may be different from each other is their **religion**. A religion is a set of beliefs. A person or a family follows and practices a religion. Protestant and Catholic are two Christian religions.

Jewish boys may wear a **yarmulke** on their heads.

Fast Fact!

The word "yarmulke" comes from the Aramaic words *yarei Malka*. This means to have reverence for the king. Wearing a yarmulke showed your faith. Now many communities require males to wear one.

Other religions include Judaism, Islam, Buddhism, and Hinduism. There are thousands of religions practiced throughout the world. Some people do not believe in any religion.

Children who practice different religions may look the same as each other. They might dress differently. Jewish boys may wear a yarmulke. A yarmulke is a small, circular cap. Muslim girls may wear a **hijab**. A

Muslim girls may wear a hijab.

Building Bridges to People Different from You

hijab is a scarf that covers a girl's hair. It may cover most of her face.

All children must be respected no matter how they dress. Learning about other children's religions is one way to be more accepting of others.

Language

Children's families may speak different languages. The children will speak English at school. Their parents may speak only the language of their homeland. At home, the children may speak Spanish, Chinese, or Russian. They may have trouble understanding English. They might speak with an **accent**.

Children can learn about others' religions or languages.

No matter how children sound or what language they speak, they should be included in any groups. They might feel different because they sound different. This is not a reason to treat them differently.

Disability

Some children have **disabilities**. They may look or act differently. They may use wheelchairs. They

Children with disabilities may need wheelchairs.

Building Bridges to People Different from You

may need extra help in the classroom if they have a learning disability.

Some students need extra help in the classroom.

Just like other children, they like to have fun. It might be harder for them to participate in games or activities. You should work harder to make sure they feel included.

Learning About Others

Children who are different might feel left out. They may wish for some children to accept them as they are. You can make them feel included. Ask them to play with you. Invite them to sit with you at lunch. Ask **polite** questions about your differences.

Opposite: Including everyone is important and fun.

Race

Children have been treated wrongly because of their race. Long ago, Native American children were forced by whites to go to **boarding schools**. They weren't allowed to speak their language. They couldn't wear their traditional clothes. They were forced to cut their hair. This was wrong. Bad things happen when people are afraid of differences.

Native American children have been mistreated at school.

Not all people who look alike are similar. Children from one country do not all like the same things. You can share an interest with anyone from anywhere. The only way to know if you do is to ask.

Children different from you may have similar interests.

We should not make **assumptions** about other children. An assumption is like a guess. You may guess wrong. You may think you won't like someone because of his or her skin color. This could be hurtful. You should give everyone a chance.

Religious Dress

Children who follow a different religion may seem scary or weird. They could wear different clothes or head wraps. This is not weird. It's just different.

You can learn about other children's religions by asking nicely.

Instead of avoiding people who are different, you can reach out. It's OK to ask questions when you notice differences. You could ask a Muslim girl about her hijab. You could ask a Jewish boy about his yarmulke. It's best to ask nicely.

KNOW YOUR NEIGHBORS

Knowing the customs of others can make them feel comfortable. In Islam, women may only shake hands with men who are close relatives. This is a form of respect. A Muslim woman in Sweden would not shake hands with a male coworker. He was offended. He did not understand her customs.

She was ordered to shake everyone's hand. This was against her religion. She quit her job because she felt uncomfortable.

It is good to be curious. It can help you learn a lot. You could get to know someone well. Then he or she will not seem so different.

Language

Children may sound different from you. They may speak another language. They may have an accent. It may be hard to understand them at times. It's important to try.

If a student speaks another language, you can learn from him or her. You may find you share interests.

It may be hard for a Spanish-speaking child to make friends. Her classmates may not understand her all the time. You can still invite her to play with you.

There is a children's book titled *Margaret and Margarita*. The two girls do not speak the same language. They still have lots of fun together.

Learning languages makes you smarter.

Building Bridges to People Different from You

Disability

Using a wheelchair is hard at school.

Many schools are not designed for children with disabilities. Students who use wheelchairs may have difficulties. Emma Albert, a teenage girl from New York City, uses a wheelchair. She has to enter the school through a back door. There is no wheelchair ramp in the front. This makes Emma feel left out.

School can be hard for children in wheelchairs. They may think they are being looked at differently. They want to have fun like everyone else. They want to be included.

You may need to be creative to include children in wheelchairs. This will be a fun challenge. You can bring everyone together. All students will feel a part of the group.

3

Diversity Activities

Maybe you have felt left out before. It's not a nice feeling. If you can include someone, he or she might not feel left out anymore.

You can do a lot to connect with people different from you. You can encourage others to do the same.

Opposite: Children are sad when they feel left out.

Culture

Everyone comes from somewhere. Your family may have lived in the United States for many **generations**. It can be exciting to learn about your

DIVERSITY BINGO

Make bingo cards with an image from a culture in each square. The image could be of a sombrero or chopsticks. There should be five squares in a row, and five rows. Make a single card to match each image on the bingo card.

The leader should hold up a single card. Each player must say what the image is and what culture it is from. The first player to get five squares right in a row—up, down, or diagonally—wins.

 Building Bridges to People Different from You

family's background. It can be fun to learn about another family's background, too.

The Walt Disney Elementary School in Mishawaka, Indiana, hosts Cultural Night. At Cultural Night, all the families come together. They celebrate their similarities and differences.

You can learn about the clothing and dances of other cultures.

You could suggest having a Cultural Night at your school. You could hear from people who speak other languages. You could try on clothing from other countries. You could try foods from other places. Dancing and music from other cultures could be included.

Children can celebrate their cultures.

You can help children from a different culture celebrate who they are.

Playing Together

Children who use wheelchairs have many challenges. It might be harder for them to move in hallways. They might have trouble sitting at a cafeteria table. They could also have trouble playing sports.

You might think it's hard to include wheelchair-using students in sports. That's not always true. Some communities host events

Wheelchair basketball is for all.

Building Bridges to People Different from You

that include everyone. Williamsport, Pennsylvania, hosts a wheelchair basketball tournament.

All the people playing are in wheelchairs. This makes the game the same for everyone. The event helps raise awareness for people with disabilities. It helps raise money for people in wheelchairs. It donates money for a ramp for their homes. You could help set up a wheelchair basketball tournament in your town. People who can walk play wheelchair basketball. This is a way to include people with disabilities.

Inclusive Classrooms

Children may also have learning disabilities. These children with disabilities have minds that work differently. They learn differently. They may get extra help from an aide. They might have a special education teacher.

Ramps allow some kids to enter their school.

Include all students in projects.

You can still be friends with them. You can include them in school projects or in games. You could help them in the classroom, too.

It might be hard for children to share their learning difficulties. You can encourage them to be themselves. School is a place for everyone to learn. You can tell them it's OK to be different.

You can also point out things they are good at. Everyone has talents. Your classmate might have trouble in math but be an excellent painter. The world is a better place because everyone has different talents.

All children have hidden and special talents.

Glossary

accent A speech pattern, tone, or way of sounding letters common to people from an area.

assumptions Things accepted as true without proof.

boarding school A school where students live away from their families.

cultures The behaviors and beliefs characteristic of a particular social, ethnic, or age group.

disabilities Physical or mental conditions that limit movements or ability to do activities.

ethnicities Social groups that share a common culture, religion, or language.

generations A group of individuals born and living around the same time.

hijab A traditional scarf worn by Muslim females.

polite Showing good manners toward others.

religion A system of attitudes, beliefs, and practices.

yarmulke A round cap worn by Jewish males.

Find Out More

Books

Lester, Julius, and Karen Barbour. *Let's Talk About Race*. New York: Amistad, 2009.

Reiser, Lynn. *Margaret and Margarita*. New York: Greenwillow, 1993.

Websites

Disability Awareness 4 You

https://disabilityawareness4you.wordpress.com/how-you-can-help

This blog provides the do's and don'ts of helping people with disabilities.

Education World

http://www.educationworld.com/a_sites/
sites053.shtml

Read the stories of different people who have immigrated to the United States and Canada.

National Wheelchair Basketball Association

http://www.nwba.org

Learn about the sport of wheelchair basketball and how you can get a team started.

Index

About the Author

Jackie F. Stanmyre is a social worker and writer. As a children's book author, she has written for the Dangerous Drugs, Game-Changing Athletes, Primary Sources of the Civil Rights Movement, and It's My State! series. Jackie lives in New Jersey with her husband and son.